CROWS

Jen Green

Grolier
an imprint of
 SCHOLASTIC
www.scholastic.com/librarypublishing

Published 2009 by Grolier
An Imprint of Scholastic Library Publishing
Old Sherman Turnpike
Danbury, Connecticut 06816

For The Brown Reference Group
Project Editor: Jolyon Goddard
Picture Researchers: Clare Newman,
Sophie Mortimer
Designer: Sarah Williams
Managing Editor: Tim Harris

Volume ISBN-13: 978-0-7172-8063-6
Volume ISBN-10: 0-7172-8063-2

**Library of Congress
Cataloging-in-Publication Data**

Nature's children. Set 6.
   p. cm.
  Includes index.
  ISBN-13: 978-0-7172-8085-8
  ISBN-10: 0-7172-8085-3
  1. Animals--Encyclopedias, Juvenile. 1.
Grolier (Firm)
  QL49.N387 2009
  590.3--dc22
                        2008014675

Printed and bound in China

PICTURE CREDITS

Front Cover: **Shutterstock**: Sharon D.

Back Cover: **Shutterstock**: Alexander
Chelmodeev, Vladimir Prusakov, RLHambley,
Normunds Rustanovics.

Corbis: W. Perry Conway 18, Nigel J. Dennis
26, Darrell Gulin 29, Eric and David Hosking
6, 21, Peter Johnson 34, Mike Jones 45,
Francesc Muntada 37, Lynda Richardson 41,
Joseph Sohm 24–25, Kennan Ward 13, Tim
Zurowski 17, 38; **NHPA**: Stephen Dalton 10,
Melvin Grey 46, E.A. Janes 30, Jany Sauvanet
42, Eric Soder 33, R. Sorensen and Jolsen 9;
Shutterstock: Sharon D 5, Ilya D. Gridnev
2–3, Al Mueller 4, Michael Woodruff 14.

Contents

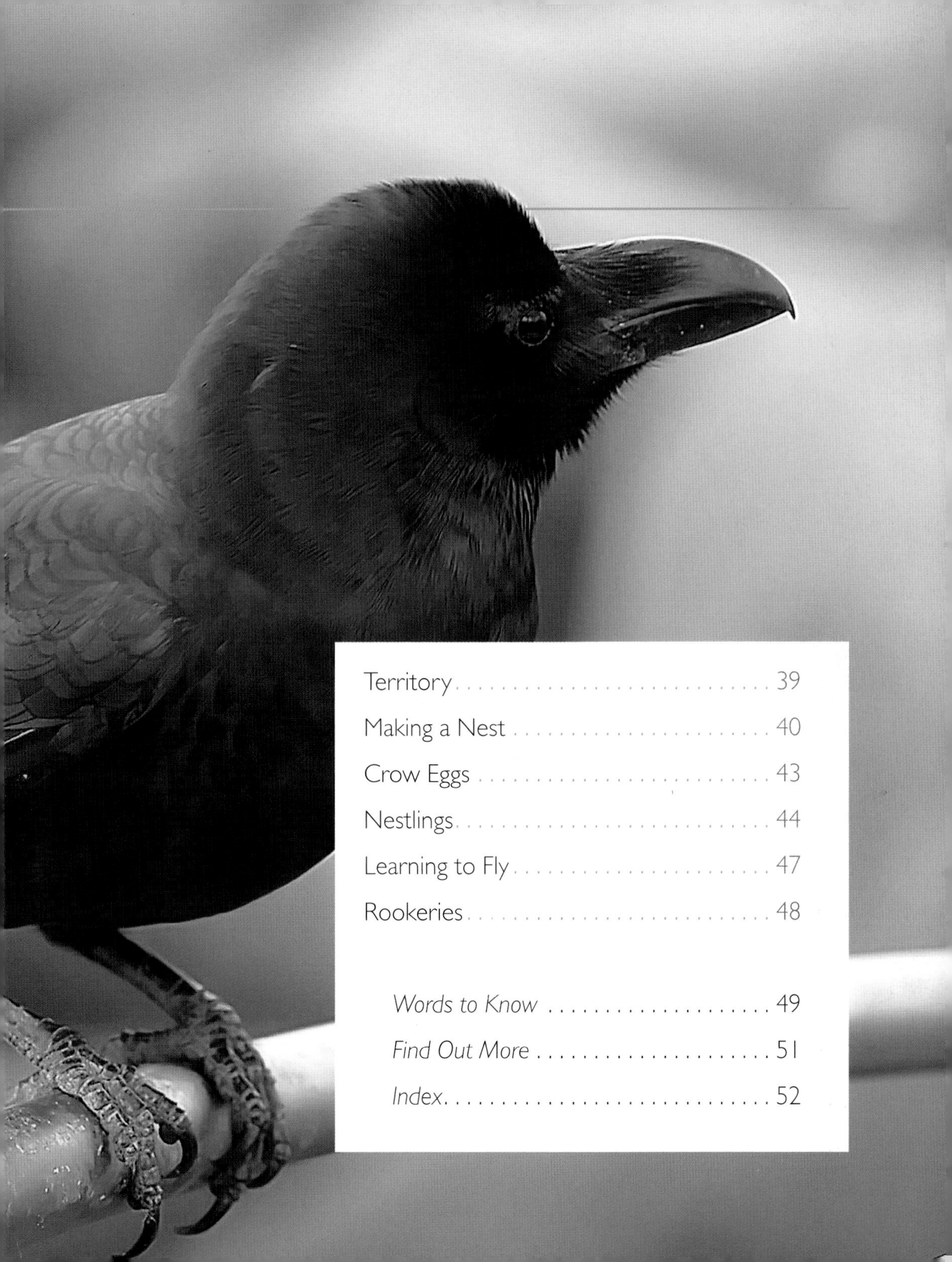

FACT FILE: Crows

Class	Birds (Aves)
Order	Songbirds (Passeriformes)
Family	Crow family (Corvidae)
Genus	Crows, ravens, and rooks (*Corvus*)
Species	There are about 40 species in the genus *Corvus*, including the American crow (*C. brachyrhynchos*) and the common raven (*C. corax*)
World distribution	Worldwide except remote islands, Antarctica, and South America
Habitat	Varies according to species; different kinds inhabit farmland, woods, towns, deserts, mountains, and tundra
Distinctive physical characteristics	Large, sturdy songbirds with dark plumage, a curving beak, and stout legs
Habits	Active in daytime; slow, deliberate flight; most crows gather in small flocks to feed; breeding pairs establish their own nesting territories
Diet	Varied; includes insects, fruit, seeds, snails, worms, small mammals, carrion, eggs, and the young of other birds

Introduction

You will often see crows in open spaces, on farms, and in woods. These big birds, with their glossy, dark **plumage**, often come into towns and cities, too. Crows are not known for the their singing abilities. Instead, they make a harsh **caw** sound. The crow family, however, is part of a group of birds known as **songbirds**. In fact, crows are the largest types of songbirds.

Crows, like parrots, are known as clever birds. Some crows use sticks as tools to dig insects out of dead wood. They sometimes even make these tools by cutting the sticks to the right length with their beak. In addition, studies have shown that some of these smart birds can count up to six!

Many people keep crows as pets.

5

Jungle crows are common all over Southeast Asia and often visit parks and gardens in search of food.

Cunning Crows

Which is the smartest bird in the world? There are several to choose from, including the talkative parrot, the wise old owl, and the racing pigeon that can find its own way home. The answer is actually the humble crow. Crows are well known for their quick wits and cunning. Myths and stories around the world celebrate their cleverness and the tricks they play.

Crows are easily tamed and make good pets, but animal lovers, beware! Crows are also famous for their love of bright, shiny objects. In fact, crows are well known thieves!

Crows are natural survivors. They do well in the wild as well as close to people in towns and cities. The secret of their success is **adaptability**. Crows fit in anywhere. Their quick thinking helps them change their habits to suit new situations.

Songbirds?

There are thousands of different **species**, or types, of birds. To help identify birds, scientists divide them into groups. The largest group, the songbirds, has more than 5,000 species.

The songbird group includes sparrows, finches, and most of the small, lively birds seen hopping about in parks and gardens. Crows are songbirds, too, but they are the heavyweights of the group. A big crow measures up to 20 inches (50 cm) long from beak to tail and weighs about 1 pound (500 g). A sparrow is less than a quarter of the crow's size. Crows are among the longest-lived birds of their group. Most songbirds live only a year or two. Many crows live into their teens—some have even been known to live for 20 years or more!

The raven, a close relative of the crow, is the largest songbird.

Patches of color help disguise a magpie's outline, making it hard to spot when perched in a tree.

The Crow Clan

Scientists group animals that are similar, but not quite the same, into animal families. True crows, such as the **carrion** crow, are not the only members of the crow family. Jays, magpies, ravens, rooks, and jackdaws are all close relatives of the true crows. In fact, the crow family is made up of more than 100 different kinds of birds.

Crows do not have bright, flashy colors, like many songbirds. Instead, they have a plain suit of black feathers and the odd patch of cream or gray. Still, crows are striking birds. Their black, glossy feathers gleam with tints of green, blue, and purple as they catch the sunlight.

Some of the small crow relatives are more colorful. Magpies are striking birds, with a black head and back, a white body, and blue wing bands. Jays often have patches of blue, green, or pink in their feathers.

Habitats

Crows have made their way to almost every corner of the globe. Some crows live thousands of feet up on the world's highest mountains. Others live in the vast, empty regions of the **Arctic**. Still others hunt for insects in the hot sands of the African deserts. Some crows settle in towns and cities, making their homes on roofs, chimneys, and towers. Others prefer to nest in dense woodlands, hidden among the trees. A few crows get the best of both town and country, shuttling between the two like commuters. During winter, they spend their days in the country, scouring the fields for food. At dusk, they fly back into the city to spend the night. That's mainly because it is warmer in the city than in the country.

Arctic crows often follow polar bears as they hunt seals. The crows steal scraps from the bears' kills.

A crow's sturdy shape allows it to survive in all kinds of environments. This crow lives in the Kalahari desert of southern Africa.

Strong Body

Birds come in many different sizes, from tiny hummingbirds to giant ostriches. Their bodies have different shapes, too, to suit their way of life. Some birds have stiltlike legs for wading in water. Others have a long, graceful neck or a strangely shaped beak that helps them eat their favorite food. Crows have none of these fancy features. Their strong, sturdy body shape is not adapted to one kind of **habitat**. Crows are at home in all kinds of places.

Like other flying birds, a crow's body is sleek and **streamlined**. This smooth shape helps the crow glide and soar through the air. Strong wings provide flapping power, while stout legs help the bird walk and hop along the ground.

Handy Tools

A crow's beak and claws come in handy when it is time to eat. The short, curving beak is used to pick tiny insects from leaves, to tug an earthworm from the ground, or to crack open the hard shell of a nut or seed. When it comes to tackling stringy meat, the crow's beak is very useful. Crows often use their claws to hold their food while they tear it into bite-sized pieces with their beak.

Beaks and claws have other uses, too. In fact, crows rely on them for everything. The crow uses its beak to clean its feathers, carry things, and build its nest. Like other songbirds, crows have four toes on each foot—three pointing forward and one pointing backward. This shape allows the bird to lock its feet around tree branches. Even when a crow is sleeping, its toes hold its **perch** tight so it won't fall.

Good balance and strong claws allow crows to rest on branches out of the reach of their enemies.

Dead animals become a feast for crows and other scavenging animals.

Varied Diet

Crows are not fussy eaters. In fact, they eat just about anything that comes their way. Seeds, fruits, and insects—especially caterpillars and beetles—are some of their favorite foods. So are juicy slugs, snails, and worms slurped up from the soil.

Crows eat larger animals, too. They hunt and kill mice, voles, and other small mammals. Carrion, the flesh of dead animals, makes an easy feast for crows.

Different crows learn special tricks to catch their favorite foods. A crow that lives by the sea may eat crabs and mussels. They drop them onto rocks from high in the air to crack open their shells. Crows from New Caledonia, in the South Pacific, are very clever. They make tools from sticks to catch grubs living in holes in dead wood. Holding the tools in their beak, these smart birds either hook out the tasty grubs or "fish" out grubs that have clamped their jaws onto the end of the tool.

Dawn Raiders

When food is scarce, crows become bold and daring. Some crows raid parks and backyards in search of scraps. Others target farms and crop fields or try their luck at garbage dumps.

Crows will also raid the nests of other birds to steal eggs or even newly hatched **chicks**. The clever crow watches the parent birds come and go to find out where their nest is hidden. The small cheeping sounds of babies calling for food can also give a nest's location away. Most nest raids are carried out at dawn. Crows may even go back to a nest a second time, when the parent birds have laid another **clutch** of eggs.

This black-backed gull's nest has been raided. Small, round holes in the eggshells are a sure sign that the clutch, or group of eggs, was eaten by a crow.

Natural Savers

Crows are natural savers. When there is plenty of food, crows are busy hoarding food for the hard times that are sure to come. Most crows hide scraps in the nooks and crannies of rocks, trees, or buildings. Some peck holes in the ground and bury their savings there. The birds remember landmarks, such as bushes, near their stored food so they can return to find it in winter.

One crow relative, the jay, takes its hoarding even further. In Canada, where the snow gets too deep for jays to bury their food, they stick nuts and seeds to the needles of fir trees, using their special sticky **saliva**.

Mischief Makers

Hoarding food is a good idea. When food is scarce, the crows rely on their hoarded food to survive. Sometimes, however, these birds hoard things they have no use for, which can lead to a lot of trouble. Crows and many of their relatives love bright, glittering objects such as pieces of foil and metal. If a crow spots a shiny object, it swoops in, snaps it up in its beak, then flies away. The crow usually then tucks the prize away in some place where it will never be seen again!

Watches, pendants, car keys—nothing that glitters in the sun is safe when these mischief makers are around. Owners of pet crows are very careful to keep their belongings hidden from their pet thieves.

Crows have well-developed eyesight and can see in color.

A pied crow stands on the back of a rhinoceros. In Africa, crows often follow large animals, snapping up the insects that buzz around them.

Clever Crows

Crows are the smarty-pants of the bird world.
When kept as pets, they learn to copy words and
phrases like parrots. They can even be taught to
find food in sealed boxes by recognizing symbols
on the lids.

Crows are good at math, too. If an egg
disappears from the nest, crow parents can
always tell. In tests, crows are able to count
up to six. No other birds have this ability.

In the wild, crows show how smart they are
by the tricks they play to steal food from other
birds. They can copy the calls of fierce hunting
birds, such as hawks and owls. They mimic the
larger birds' calls to scare smaller birds away.
No scarecrow, guarding the farmer's field of
seeds or crops, will fool these smart birds for
long. Crows even raid traps set to catch them,
stealing the bait without getting caught!

Feathers

An adult crow has more than 3,000 black, glossy feathers that cover it from head to toe. These feathers include fluffy **down** feathers, which keep the crow's body warm, and long, stiff flight feathers, which allow the birds to fly.

Maintaining healthy feathers is a lot of work. A crow must clean its feathers every day to keep them trim and tidy. Whenever it has a spare moment, a crow combs and nibbles at its feathers with its beak. This is called **preening**.

Once or twice a year, a crow sheds, or **molts**, its feathers. One by one, the old feathers drop out, and shiny new ones grow in their place.

A crow's flight feather is made up of a hollow central shaft that supports a fine mesh of fibers, called a web, on each side.

The shallow water at the edge of a pond or stream is an ideal bathing spot for crows.

Staying Clean

Crows take regular baths to rinse their feathers. Like other birds, they also take dust baths, showering themselves with dirt to get rid of pests, such as lice, that live in their feathers.

Crows also have some unusual bathing habits not shared by other birds. They are sometimes seen perched on anthills with their wings outstretched, letting the ants crawl all over their body! Experts think the ants spray stinging acid onto the feathers, which helps kill lice and bugs.

In cities, crows sit on smoking chimneys and spread their feathers in the gray, billowing clouds of smoke. The smoke is thought to kill bugs living on the bird.

As the Crow Flies

Crows are not the fastest fliers of the bird world, but they are steady. They flap along at an even 30 miles (50 km) per hour. Some birds bob and dip in the air as they fly. Crows take a straight line to their destination. When they don't have anywhere to get to, crows can be playful and acrobatic in the air, wheeling and swooping just for the fun of it. Male crows show off in the air to impress their **mates**.

Flying allows birds to escape from enemies and seek out food beyond the reach of other animals. But it can be exhausting. Flapping across the backyard takes more than ten times as much energy as walking the same distance.

Crows save energy in flight by riding the currents of warm air that swirl around crags, cliffs, and hills.

A brave crow flies just
out of reach behind
a black eagle and
squawks to alert its
flock to the danger.

Flock Together

Most crows are sociable birds. They are often found together in **flocks** of a dozen or more. At dusk, the flock collects to find a safe place to **roost**, or sleep, through the night. As the sun rises, crows gather in the fields to feed. A flock of crows, searching with many pairs of eyes, has a much better chance of spotting food than just one bird alone. If the flock comes upon a rich supply of food, there will be quite a party!

Crows also feed in flocks because it is safer. Each bird acts as a lookout. If a prowling cat approaches, one member of the flock will be sure to spot the danger, alerting the others to fly away. Once in the air, a flock of wheeling crows can confuse an enemy such as a hawk or eagle. In the mass of fluttering bodies, the hunter finds it hard to pick out a single victim and might miss them all.

Noisy Birds

Crows are songbirds, but they are not sweet singers! The most these birds can manage is a hoarse, croaking call. Many of the crow's relatives are named after the sound they make. A blue jay introduces itself by calling "jay-jay." Crows go "kraa," choughs (CHUFFS) say "tchuff," while jackdaws repeat their name, "chak-chak," for all to hear.

Crows are noisy birds and call to one another a lot. Birds feeding in a flock caw softly to keep the group together. If danger threatens, a loud, harsh squawk sounds the alarm for the whole flock. Crows also use their calls like passwords to identify themselves. Birds of the same flock know one another's calls, and parent birds recognize the voices of their children anywhere.

The pied crow's harsh calls can be heard in grasslands all over Africa.

A pair of American crows keeps watch over their territory.

Territory

Like other birds, crows pair up to have young. Many kinds of birds pair up only for a season, but crows are loyal. When a male and female become partners, their union lasts for life. The male crow does a special dance to court the female. He bows and dips to his lady, then fluffs up his feathers and struts around.

At the start of the **breeding season**, a pair of crows celebrates their union by leaving the flock and making themselves a **territory**. A territory is a patch of land where they will hunt for food and bring up young. They patrol the borders of their patch so other birds know they should keep away. Once a patch is won, the pair will defend it against strangers. Squirrels, other birds, even local cats, all are chased away!

Making a Nest

Crows make a nest not to sleep in but as a home for their young. The nest is a warm, snug place for the babies to grow up. Most crows build their nest perched in the fork of a bush or tree. Others nest in chimneys, on rooftops, or in holes in cliffs.

To start a nest, crows gather sticks and twigs. The first sticks must be firmly placed, like house foundations, or the nest will be unsteady. This can be tricky for the crows that nest in chimneys. Often a huge pile of twigs is dropped down a chimney before one stick wedges firmly enough to start the nest!

When the twigs are in place, the female hollows out the inside of the nest. She lines it with soft moss, grass, wool, and hairs. Nests are sometimes finished with a roof of sharp thorns to keep enemies—like other crows—away.

A crow picks up a feather to add to its nest.

Crows lay up to nine eggs in each clutch.

Crow Eggs

Once the nest is finished, the female lays her eggs. Crows lay just one batch of eggs each year. The eggs, which are pale blue or green in color, have a covering of dark speckles that helps hide them among the dappled leaves. Inside the hard shells, the chicks develop. The mother sits on her eggs to keep them warm. While she sits patiently, her mate brings her food. Then the mate takes a turn sitting on the eggs when she needs a break. After two to three weeks, the eggs are ready to hatch. Each baby bird pecks a line of holes in its shell with the help of a bony knob on its beak, called the **egg tooth**. It then forces its shell apart and struggles free.

Nestlings

Newly hatched baby crows are a sorry sight. Their bald, pink body has no feathers, and the little birds are blind. Weak and helpless, they cannot stand up or feed themselves. Instead, in their first weeks of life the **nestlings** rely on their mother and father for everything. The grown-ups are kept busy all day long, flying back and forth collecting food for their hungry young. When they hear their parents coming, the babies open their beaks wide and cheep for food. Very young chicks are fed coughed-up food that the parents have already partly digested. As the chicks get older, their parents drop insects, worms, and caterpillars into their gaping mouths—and there's always room for more!

The babies need water to drink, too. So their parents fly to a nearby pond or stream and soak themselves. Their down feathers hold water like a sponge. Once back at the nest, the chicks suck the water from their parents' feathers to get a refreshing drink.

Looking after chicks is a full-time job for both parents.

Soon this young crow must leave the safety of its nest forever.

Learning to Fly

On a rich diet of insects and worms, the baby birds grow quickly. Soon their first feathers sprout, and they can clamber around the nest. It isn't long before they are ready to leave the safety of their home. About a month after hatching, it is time for the baby crows to test out their wings. The young crows launch into the air for the first time.

At first, the babies are clumsy and unsteady in the air. They rest in the bushes out of sight and beg for food from their parents. Soon, they are strong enough to hop after their parents, cheeping eagerly. For the next few weeks, they stay close to their parents. The whole family roams the countryside in search of food. The young birds are now almost fully grown. By watching their parents, they learn the skills they need to survive on their own.

Rookeries

Pairs of crows go off on their own to raise a family, but their relatives—the rooks—nest in special **colonies** called rookeries or rook cities. A rook city is unmistakable—a group of large, untidy nests perched high in a clump of tall trees. The same site is used for years by generations of rooks. A large rookery may house as many as 9,000 birds!

Each pair of rooks has its own nest, but the nests are mostly rebuilt from year to year rather than started fresh. In spring the parents-to-be steal twigs from their neighbors' nests to repair their home! The rookery is a noisy place, as rooks squabble over twigs and shoo away neighbors that come too close.

Words to Know

Adaptability — The ability to change in order to survive new conditions.

Arctic — The cold, icy region around the North Pole.

Breeding season — The time of the year when animals come together to produce young.

Carrion — The flesh of dead animals.

Caw — The call made by crows.

Chicks — Young birds.

Clutch — A batch, or set, of eggs.

Colonies — Groups of birds that nest together.

Down — Soft, fluffy feathers.

Egg tooth — A toothlike projection at the end of a chick's beak used to help it hatch.

Flocks — Groups of birds.

Habitat — The type of place where an animal or plant lives.

Mates — Breeding partners.

49

Molts	Sheds old feathers to replace them with new ones.
Nestlings	Baby birds that still live in the nest and cannot yet fly.
Perch	A resting place for a bird.
Plumage	A bird's feathers.
Preening	Cleaning and combing the feathers.
Roost	To find a place to sleep at night; a place in which a bird sleeps.
Saliva	A fluid produced in an animal's mouth that helps digest food.
Songbirds	The largest group of birds, to which the crow family belongs.
Species	The scientific word for animals of the same kind that breed together.
Streamlined	Describes a smooth, sleek shape that moves through air or water easily.
Territory	The area in which an animal or group of animals lives and often defends from other animals.

Find Out More

Books

Lunis, N., and M. Goldish. *Crows*. Smart Animals. New York: Bearport Publishing, 2005.

Pringle, L. P. *Crows! Strange and Wonderful*. Honesdale, Pennsylvania: Boyds Mills Press, 2002.

Web sites

American Crow
www.enchantedlearning.com/subjects/birds/printouts/Crowprintout.shtml
Information about the American crow and a picture to print and color in.

Crow Invasion
video.nationalgeographic.com/video/player/kids/animals-pets-kids/wild-detectives-kids/wd-ep7-crowinvasion.html
Watch a short film about a town invaded by crows.

Index